Kathryn Kratoff

Eleanor Schick

MY ALBUM

GREENWILLOW BOOKS, NEW YORK

Library of Congress Cataloging in Publication Data
Schick, Eleanor, (date)   My album.
Summary: A young writer describes herself
and her family in her journal.
[1. Diaries—Fiction]   I. Title.
PZ7.S3445My 1984   [E]   83-25420
ISBN 0-688-03827-1
ISBN 0-688-03828-X (lib. bdg.)

For my brother, Michael

Contents

 My mother has brown eyes. My father has brown eyes. I have brown eyes too.

My mother's hair is wavy and black. My father's hair is curly and brown. My hair is wavy like my mother's, and brown like my father's.

I have a brother Carl, and a sister Julie. They have brown eyes too.

Their hair is blond, like Grandpa Joseph's, and very curly.

2 My sister Julie loves bright colors. She keeps green plants on her windowsill, on a red mat.

She wears bright blouses, and ribbons in her hair. She embroiders pretty patches and sews them on her bluejeans.

When the sun goes down each night, she stops doing her homework just long enough to watch the colors turning orange, and then purple, and then dark. Sometimes she calls me in to see.

I asked Julie to help me put bright colors in my room. We chose a yellow bedspread for my bed, and red curtains for my window. We put a bright green plant on my windowsill.

Now I watch the sun go down through my red curtains.

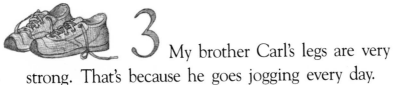 My brother Carl's legs are very strong. That's because he goes jogging every day. I like his strong legs.

I like Sunday afternoons because Carl takes me jogging with him.

We jog across town, and under the bridge, and all the way to the lake. We skip stones, or we rest under the trees. Then we walk home. We pick up pretty rocks along the way and save them for our collection.

We keep it in a cardboard box at the bottom of my closet.

I like the way my legs are growing strong, like Carl's.

 My father reads the newspaper each day. I think he reads every word. On Sunday mornings, he sits in his favorite chair with the light coming over his shoulder, and he reads the whole Sunday paper. I sit on the floor, on the rug, and read the comics.

I like being with him, not talking. He has a way of just being near, and making the whole room peaceful.

I like being quiet, like my father.

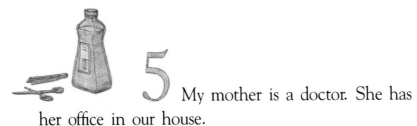

5 My mother is a doctor. She has her office in our house.

When I get home from school, I have to be very quiet so I won't disturb her. Sometimes my mother comes out of her office to say hello to me and ask about my day in school. Then she goes back to work.

Whenever I'm sick, or hurt, my mother knows what to do. Once I got a splinter under my nail that no one else could get out.

My mother cleaned my finger with alcohol and cut my nail very short. Then she took the splinter out with a tweezer.

It hurt, and I cried, and Julie had to hold me still. But when it was all over, the hurting stopped.

Maybe, someday, I'll be a doctor. Then I can help people when they're sick, or hurt.

6 My Uncle Bob is an artist. I love to visit his studio. When he opens the door, I smell the oil paints and the turpentine. I like the big window, and the light flooding in, and the paintings hanging everywhere. I like the fruit, and the dishes, and the flowers he has on all his tables. I like his old, comfortable chairs, and the brushes and paints, and statues everywhere. I like the clothes Uncle Bob wears. I like the way he's never in a hurry. I like Uncle Bob.

Uncle Bob says he'll give me painting lessons if I practice drawing. I put fruits, and dishes, and flowers on my table, and I draw them. I draw the shapes, and the shadows, the way Uncle Bob told me to.

Maybe, someday, I'll be an artist.

 **7** My cousin Allison is a dancer. On my birthday, she took me to the ballet to see *Swan Lake*. I wore my favorite dress.

Allison says that the dancers make us feel the music. Allison loves *Swan Lake*. So do I.

When it was over, Allison bought me a record of the music. Now I play the record in our living room. It's the forest, and I'm the Swan Queen.

Maybe, someday, I'll be a dancer.

21

8　　There's a lady who lives next door to us, named Loretta. Loretta's house looks old-fashioned. It's the same one she lived in when she was young, and she never changed anything, not even the furniture.

Loretta says she was born there.

Sometimes I visit Loretta in the afternoons, when I get home from school. She always has a piece of home-baked raisin cake for me, and a glass of milk with molasses.

Loretta lives alone with her cat, Buttons. Buttons sits on Loretta's lap and purrs while Loretta talks to me. I think Buttons is Loretta's best friend.

Someday, when I'm very old, if I live alone like Loretta, I'm going to have a cat, and I'll name him Buttons.

 My teacher in school is Mr. Sanchez. Mr. Sanchez gives us special homework once a week. He calls it our journal.

We have to write something about what we see, or think, or feel. It can be very short, or it can be a whole page long. He says it doesn't matter how long it is, but it has to be true.

I like our journal homework. That's why I'm starting a journal of my own, at home. I write in it every day. I write about what I think, and feel. Sometimes I write private things that I wouldn't show Mr. Sanchez, or anybody.

I think I will keep writing in my journal all my life.

10 My Grandma Juanita makes all her clothing, and she sews it all by hand. She says her mother taught her to sew when she was young, like me.

When I was a baby, Grandma Juanita made me a rag doll. That's the doll I used to take everywhere I went, when I was little. I named her Tracy. Now Tracy stays home, but I sleep with her at night.

Grandma Juanita is teaching me to sew. We're making a pleated skirt for me. Grandma Juanita does the cutting and the pinning, and she's teaching me to do the stitching. We're sewing it by hand.

Someday, I'm going to make all kinds of clothes for myself, and I'm going to design them too.

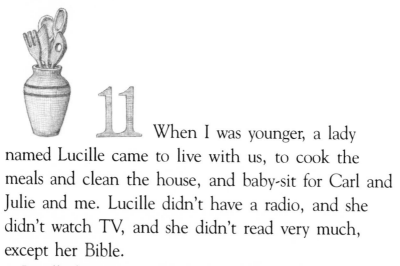

When I was younger, a lady named Lucille came to live with us, to cook the meals and clean the house, and baby-sit for Carl and Julie and me. Lucille didn't have a radio, and she didn't watch TV, and she didn't read very much, except her Bible.

Lucille hummed while she worked, and she prayed out loud when she went to bed. She was always very kind to me.

Carl and Julie and I are older now. We take care of each other when no one else is home, and we help with the housework. That's why Lucille doesn't live with us anymore.

Now when I wash the dishes or help clean the house, I hum to myself, and I think of Lucille.

I will always remember her.

 My Grandma Celia saves things that remind her of special times. She has a composition that she wrote in school which was published in the newspaper. She has her high school graduation picture. She has letters that my mother wrote to her when she went away to camp. She has photographs of the family from before my mother was born.

Sometimes Grandma Celia takes them out to look at, and remember. Sometimes she tells me stories about them, of the olden days.

I'm starting to collect special things too. I have the program from *Swan Lake*. I have all my favorite drawings. I have a pressed flower and a four-leaf clover. I have a journal homework paper that Mr. Sanchez wrote A + on, in red pencil.

I want to save them all my life.

Maybe, someday, I'll have grandchildren and I'll show them the things I've saved, and tell them stories of the olden days.

Young Writers
in our city